GLORY TO GOD IN THE HIGHEST

GLORY TO GOD IN THE HIGHEST

CHRISTMAS READINGS FROM THE OLD AND NEW TESTAMENTS WITH REFLECTIONS

MICHAEL JAMES FITZGERALD

OVERDUE BOOKS

Printed in the United States of America.

Third Edition, November 2013 (rev. 20191214)

To be read from December 1 through December 31.

All verses taken from the King James Version, first published in AD 1611.

ISBN-10: 1-887309-18-7

ISBN-13: 978-1-887309-18-9

Cover art: "The Shepherds and the Angel" (1879) by Danish artist Carl Bloch (1834–1890). Public domain.

CONTENTS

INTRODUCTION

This little volume was created to help you focus on Jesus Christ during the Christmas season. These Christmas readings and devotionals highlight 31 passages of scripture from the Old and New Testaments (King James Version). They can be read each day during the month of December.

Every passage is followed by a short reflection to help you meditate on the meaning of the verses and to discuss them with family or friends. May these readings help you draw closer to our Savior this Christmas season and many seasons to come.

DECEMBER 1

❦

UNTIL SHILOH COME

*T*he sceptre shall not depart from Judah, nor a lawgiver from between his feet, until Shiloh come; and unto him shall the gathering of the people be.

Genesis 49:10

This is one of the earliest recorded prophecies of our Savior, Jesus Christ. *Shiloh* in Hebrew means "peaceful one," the One unto whom "the gathering of the people [will] be." How has Christ been the Peaceful One in your life?

DECEMBER 2

∝≫

IMMANUEL

*T*herefore the Lord himself shall give you a sign; Behold, a virgin shall conceive, and bear a son, and shall call his name Immanuel.

Isaiah 7:14

From Hebrew, the name *Immanuel* means "God with us." Some days it's difficult to know when God is with us. He *is* always there, waiting for your simple prayer, "Lord, I need your help." How can we be *with Him* today?

Consider singing or listening to the traditional carol "O Come, O Come, Emmanuel."

DECEMBER 3

THE PRINCE OF PEACE

*F*or unto us a child is born, unto us a son is given: and the government shall be upon his shoulder: and his name shall be called Wonderful, Counsellor, The mighty God, The everlasting Father, The Prince of Peace.

Of the increase of his government and peace there shall be no end, upon the throne of David, and upon his kingdom, to order it, and to establish it with judgment and with justice from henceforth even for ever. The zeal of the LORD of hosts will perform this.

Isaiah 9:6–7

Jesus Christ is called "Counseller" in this passage. The question is, are we willing to follow His counsel? How much better, how much more peaceful might our lives be if we followed His wise counsel today and each day of our lives?

Consider listening to "For unto Us a Child Is Born" from Handel's *Messiah*.

DECEMBER 4

✁

BEHOLD YOUR GOD!

O Zion, that bringest good tidings, get thee up into the high mountain; O Jerusalem, that bringest good tidings, lift up thy voice with strength; lift it up, be not afraid; say unto the cities of Judah, Behold your God!

Behold, the Lord GOD will come with strong hand, and his arm shall rule for him: behold, his reward is with him, and his work before him.

He shall feed his flock like a shepherd: he shall gather the lambs with his arm, and carry them in his bosom, and shall gently lead those that are with young.

Isaiah 40:9–11

What keeps us from seeing and beholding the majesty of Jesus Christ each day? What keeps us from having the humility to let Him "gently lead" us?

Consider listening to "O Thou That Tellest Good Tidings to Zion" from Handel's *Messiah*.

DECEMBER 5

RULER IN ISRAEL

*B*ut thou, Beth-lehem Ephratah, though thou be little among the thousands of Judah, yet out of thee shall he come forth unto me that is to be ruler in Israel; whose goings forth have been from of old, from everlasting.

Micah 5:2

This prophecy tells us that Jesus will be born in Bethlehem, as prophesied by Micah eight centuries before His birth. In Hebrew, Bethlehem means "house of bread." In that light, recall that Christ called Himself the Bread of Life (see John 6:35).

Consider singing or listening to the traditional carol "Oh Little Town of Bethlehem."

DECEMBER 6

❦

THE DESIRE OF ALL NATIONS

For thus saith the LORD of hosts; Yet once, it is a little while, and I will shake the heavens, and the earth, and the sea, and the dry land;

And I will shake all nations, and the desire of all nations shall come: and I will fill this house with glory, saith the LORD of hosts.

Haggai 2:6–7

Haggai calls Jesus "the desire of all nations." How can we receive our greatest, most worthy desire with His help?

DECEMBER 7

❧

BLESSED ART THOU AMONG WOMEN

*A*nd in the sixth month the angel Gabriel was sent from God unto a city of Galilee, named Nazareth,

To a virgin espoused to a man whose name was Joseph, of the house of David; and the virgin's name was Mary.

And the angel came in unto her, and said, Hail, thou that art highly favoured, the Lord is with thee: blessed art thou among women.

And when she saw him, she was troubled at his saying, and cast in her mind what manner of salutation this should be.

Luke 1:26–29

Have you ever been given a duty or responsibility that came as a shock to you? What was your reaction then? What would it be now? How do you think Mary really felt when the angel Gabriel delivered this surprising announcement?

Consider listening to the traditional Basque carol "Gabriel's Message."

DECEMBER 8

⁂

THE SON OF THE HIGHEST

*A*nd the angel said unto her, Fear not, Mary: for thou hast found favour with God.

And, behold, thou shalt conceive in thy womb, and bring forth a son, and shalt call his name JESUS.

He shall be great, and shall be called the Son of the Highest: and the Lord God shall give unto him the throne of his father David:

And he shall reign over the house of Jacob for ever; and of his kingdom there shall be no end.

Luke 1:30–33

The Son of the Highest will reign over Israel forever and His kingdom shall have no end. Someday, perhaps not long from now, He will return to earth, dismiss all self-appointed regents, and take the kingdom that is rightfully His.

Consider listening to the Hallelujah Chorus from Handel's *Messiah*.

DECEMBER 9

THE POWER OF THE HIGHEST

*T*hen said Mary unto the angel, How shall this be, seeing I know not a man?

And the angel answered and said unto her, The Holy Ghost shall come upon thee, and the power of the Highest shall overshadow thee: therefore also that holy thing which shall be born of thee shall be called the Son of God.

And, behold, thy cousin Elisabeth, she hath also conceived a son in her old age: and this is the sixth month with her, who was called barren.

For with God nothing shall be impossible.

Luke 1:34–37

If nothing is impossible with God, what is possible for us? What or who makes things impossible?

DECEMBER 10

BEHOLD THE HANDMAID OF THE LORD

*A*nd Mary said, Behold the handmaid of the Lord; be it unto me according to thy word. And the angel departed from her.

Luke 1:38

Facing challenges takes inner strength and commitment. Most of us have faced challenges we had no idea how to handle, but with the help of heaven, we found a way.How can we develop faith to live by these words, "Lord, be it unto me according to your word"?

DECEMBER 11

⚜

FILLED WITH THE HOLY GHOST

*A*nd Mary arose in those days, and went into the hill country with haste, into a city of Juda;

And entered into the house of Zacharias, and saluted Elisabeth.

And it came to pass, that, when Elisabeth heard the salutation of Mary, the babe leaped in her womb; and Elisabeth was filled with the Holy Ghost:

Luke 1:39–41

Elisabeth was filled with the Holy Ghost when Mary arrived, an affirmation that the Child Mary bore was divine. Have you ever experienced a divine affirmation? Have you shared it with others?

DECEMBER 12

❦

THE BABE LEAPED

*A*nd she [Elisabeth] spake out with a loud voice, and said, Blessed art thou among women, and blessed is the fruit of thy womb.

And whence is this to me, that the mother of my Lord should come to me?

For, lo, as soon as the voice of thy salutation sounded in mine ears, the babe leaped in my womb for joy.

And blessed is she that believed: for there shall be a performance of those things which were told her from the Lord.

Luke 1:42–45

How did Elisabeth know about Mary's special calling? Why was it important or even critical that Elizabeth shared her witness with Mary? How could it have strengthened Mary?

DECEMBER 13

❧

ALL GENERATIONS SHALL CALL ME BLESSED

*A*nd Mary said, My soul doth magnify the Lord,
And my spirit hath rejoiced in God my Saviour.
For he hath regarded the low estate of his handmaiden: for, behold, from henceforth all generations shall call me blessed.

Luke 1:46–48

Can you remember a time when your soul magnified the Lord? When did that happen and why was it special to you? Have you written this down and have you shared it with others?

Consider listening to J. S. Bach's *Magnificat*.

DECEMBER 14

❧

HE HATH SCATTERED THE PROUD

For he that is mighty hath done to me great things; and holy is his name.

And his mercy is on them that fear him from generation to generation.

He hath shewed strength with his arm; he hath scattered the proud in the imagination of their hearts.

Luke 1:49–51

God resists the proud but gives grace to the humble (see James 4:6). He respects the lowly (see Psalms 138:6) but scatters the proud "in the imagination of their hearts." How and why does God love and protect the humble?

DECEMBER 15

HE HATH FILLED THE HUNGRY

He hath put down the mighty from their seats, and exalted them of low degree.

He hath filled the hungry with good things; and the rich he hath sent empty away.

He hath holpen [helped] his servant Israel, in remembrance of his mercy;

As he spake to our fathers, to Abraham, and to his seed for ever.

And Mary abode with her [Elisabeth] about three months, and returned to her own house.

Luke 1:52–56

Those in "low degree" in this world are held in high regard by God. Why does he protect and help them? How does He exalt them and lift them up?

DECEMBER 16

✌

SHE WAS FOUND WITH CHILD

*N*ow the birth of Jesus Christ was on this wise: When as his mother Mary was espoused to Joseph, before they came together, she was found with child of the Holy Ghost.

Then Joseph her husband, being a just man, and not willing to make her a publick example, was minded to put her away privily.

Matthew 1:18–19

Why do we often struggle to understand the Lord's will in our lives? Can setting our doubts aside for a higher cause free us to do great things in the world? Once we wrestle with and subdue our doubts, can they lead us to strength and victory?

DECEMBER 17

❦

HE SHALL SAVE HIS PEOPLE

*B*ut while he thought on these things, behold, the angel of the Lord appeared unto him in a dream, saying, Joseph, thou son of David, fear not to take unto thee Mary thy wife: for that which is conceived in her is of the Holy Ghost.

And she shall bring forth a son, and thou shalt call his name JESUS: for he shall save his people from their sins.

Matthew 1:20–21

God placed tremendous trust in Joseph. He was commanded to "fear not" to take Mary as his wife even though Joseph knew he wasn't the father of her Child. Why did the angel appear to Joseph "while he thought on these things"? How did he find the courage and faith to overcome his doubt and become the earthly father and protector of the Son of God?

DECEMBER 18

GOD WITH US

*N*ow all this was done, that it might be fulfilled which was spoken of the Lord by the prophet [Isaiah 7:14], saying,

Behold, a virgin shall be with child, and shall bring forth a son, and they shall call his name Emmanuel, which being interpreted is, God with us.

Matthew 1:22–23

How could the prophet Isaiah accurately predict the birth of Christ? Who helps prophets see and know the truth about the future? How can their prophecies help us personally?

DECEMBER 19

❦

HE CALLED HIS NAME JESUS

*T*hen Joseph being raised from sleep did as the angel of the Lord had bidden him, and took unto him his wife: And knew her not till she had brought forth her firstborn son: and he called his name JESUS.

Matthew 1:24–25

Mary's divine son was named Jesus, as foretold by the angel Gabriel (see Luke 1:31). The Greek name *Jesus* is a translation of the Hebrew *Yeshua* or *Joshua* which means Deliverer, Rescuer, or Savior. Take a moment to ponder the ways Jesus has delivered, rescued, and saved you and those around you.

DECEMBER 20

A DECREE FROM CAESAR AUGUSTUS

*A*nd it came to pass in those days, that there went out a decree from Caesar Augustus, that all the world should be taxed.

(And this taxing was first made when Cyrenius was governor of Syria.)

And all went to be taxed, every one into his own city.

And Joseph also went up from Galilee, out of the city of Nazareth, into Judaea, unto the city of David, which is called Bethlehem; (because he was of the house and lineage of David:)

To be taxed with Mary his espoused wife, being great with child.

Luke 2:1–5

How through this event of a tax enrollment or census did the Lord bring about the fulfillment of an extraordinary, prophetic event?

Consider singing or listening to the traditional carol "O Little Town of Bethlehem."

DECEMBER 21

HER FIRSTBORN SON

*A*nd so it was, that, while they were there, the days were accomplished that she should be delivered.

And she brought forth her firstborn son, and wrapped him in swaddling clothes, and laid him in a manger; because there was no room for them in the inn.

Luke 2:6–7

Perhaps there have been times—as with most of us—when you haven't made the Savior welcome in your life. How did you get past that season? How can you make Jesus more welcome and present in your life now?

❦

THE GLORY OF THE LORD

*A*nd there were in the same country shepherds abiding in the field, keeping watch over their flock by night.

And, lo, the angel of the Lord came upon them, and the glory of the Lord shone round about them: and they were sore afraid.

Luke 2:8–9

Why do the humble and lowly received great gifts and privileges from God? Why did the angel appear to the shepherds rather than to the popular religious and political leaders of the time?

Consider singing or listening to the traditional carol "While Shepherds Watched Their Flocks."

DECEMBER 23

 ∞

GOOD TIDINGS OF GREAT JOY

*A*nd the angel said unto them, Fear not: for, behold, I bring you good tidings of great joy, which shall be to all people.

For unto you is born this day in the city of David a Saviour, which is Christ the Lord.

And this shall be a sign unto you; Ye shall find the babe wrapped in swaddling clothes, lying in a manger.

Luke 2:10–12

Why was the news of the birth of Jesus "good tidings of great joy . . . to *all* people"? What did His first coming to earth mean to the Jewish nation and other nations of the earth?

DECEMBER 24

ON EARTH PEACE

*A*nd suddenly there was with the angel a multitude of the heavenly host praising God, and saying,

Glory to God in the highest, and on earth peace, good will toward men.

And it came to pass, as the angels were gone away from them into heaven, the shepherds said one to another, Let us now go even unto Bethlehem, and see this thing which is come to pass, which the Lord hath made known unto us.

Luke 2:13–15

How can we help Christ bring peace on earth and "good will toward men" today? Where can we start and how can we begin?

Consider singing or listening to the traditional carol "Hark! The Herald Angels Sing."

DECEMBER 25

❧

AND THEY CAME WITH HASTE

*A*nd they came with haste, and found Mary, and Joseph, and the babe lying in a manger.

And when they had seen it, they made known abroad the saying which was told them concerning this child.

And all they that heard it wondered at those things which were told them by the shepherds.

But Mary kept all these things, and pondered them in her heart.

And the shepherds returned, glorifying and praising God for all the things that they had heard and seen, as it was told unto them.

Luke 2:16–20

Why did the shepherds come "with haste" to see the Christ Child? How can we personally make "known abroad" the wonderful story of Jesus Christ? How can we make our message personal and meaningful as we share it with others?

Consider singing or listening to the traditional carol "Silent Night."

DECEMBER 26

❧

WE HAVE SEEN HIS STAR

*N*ow when Jesus was born in Bethlehem of Judaea in the days of Herod the king, behold, there came wise men from the east to Jerusalem,

Saying, Where is he that is born King of the Jews? for we have seen his star in the east, and are come to worship him.

When Herod the king had heard these things, he was troubled, and all Jerusalem with him.

And when he had gathered all the chief priests and scribes of the people together, he demanded of them where Christ should be born.

Matthew 2:1–4

Why did the wise men come from the east to Jerusalem and why did their arrival trouble and even threaten Herod? Why does Jesus' mission sometimes trouble people today?

Consider singing or listening to the traditional hymn "With Wondering Awe."

DECEMBER 27

A GOVERNOR

*A*nd they said unto him, In Bethlehem of Judaea: for thus it is written by the prophet,

And thou Bethlehem, in the land of Juda, art not the least among the princes of Juda: for out of thee shall come a Governor, that shall rule my people Israel [see Micah 5:2].

Then Herod, when he had privily called the wise men, enquired of them diligently what time the star appeared.

And he sent them to Bethlehem, and said, Go and search diligently for the young child; and when ye have found him, bring me word again, that I may come and worship him also.

Matthew 2:5–8

Sometimes our outward goodness does not match what we feel inside. How can we shape our hearts to match the good ways we know we should live?

DECEMBER 28

☙

THE STAR

*W*hen they had heard the king, they departed; and, lo, the star, which they saw in the east, went before them, till it came and stood over where the young child was.

When they saw the star, they rejoiced with exceeding great joy.

Matthew 2:9–10

How can we personally follow the star back to Jesus Christ? Is it there even though we can't see it? Who or what represents the star to you?

DECEMBER 29

⚜

THEY PRESENTED UNTO HIM GIFTS

*A*nd when they were come into the house, they saw the young child with Mary his mother, and fell down, and worshipped him: and when they had opened their treasures, they presented unto him gifts; gold, and frankincense, and myrrh.

Matthew 2:11

How did these gifts help Jesus and His family as they traveled to Egypt? What precious and helpful gifts can we give Jesus now as we give to others?

DECEMBER 30

BEING WARNED OF GOD

*A*nd being warned of God in a dream that they should not return to Herod, they departed into their own country another way.

And when they were departed, behold, the angel of the Lord appeareth to Joseph in a dream, saying, Arise, and take the young child and his mother, and flee into Egypt, and be thou there until I bring thee word: for Herod will seek the young child to destroy him.

Matthew 2:12–13

Be divine means, God gave the wise men and Joseph warnings to flee from the evil intent of a wicked king. Is there anything in your life right now that you've been warned to flee?

DECEMBER 31

❧

OUT OF EGYPT HAVE I CALLED MY SON

*W*hen he arose, he took the young child and his mother by night, and departed into Egypt:

And was there until the death of Herod: that it might be fulfilled which was spoken of the Lord by the prophet, saying, Out of Egypt have I called my son.

Matthew 2:14–15

Like Christ, the Lord calls us "out of Egypt" (see Hosea 11:1). Egypt could represent the corrupt world we live in now. How can we live in a corrupt world but also escape it?

AFTERWORD

For centuries before His birth, Christ's life was foretold by prophets. Surely, as the scriptures testify, He was the long-promised Messiah. His life is a message to all of us to repent and serve God, to be humble, generous, forgiving, and kind, to love and help others, to look up and seek His grace. May this and every Christmas season remind us to find room for Him in our hearts and lives.

www.ingramcontent.com/pod-product-compliance
Lightning Source LLC
Chambersburg PA
CBHW030310030426
42337CB00012B/664